THE Will Ackerman COLLECTION

Music transcriptions by Nick Stasinos and Pete Billman

Cover Photo by Jeff Baird
Used by permission

ISBN 0-634-01179-0

7777 W. BLUEMOUND RD. P.O. BOX 13819 MILWAUKEE, WI 53213

For all works contained herein:
Unauthorized copying, arranging, adapting, recording or public performance is an infringement of copyright.
Infringers are liable under the law.

Visit Hal Leonard Online at
www.halleonard.com

Photo by John Cooper

Photo by Bill Reitzel

A NOTE

I've had the honor of signing to my record label and producing guitarists of the caliber of Alex deGrassi and Michael Hedges, among others. Inevitably, I was tempted on occasion to transform my own guitars into kindling. I'm glad that didn't come to pass as I've received many letters over the years telling me that my melodies have reached people on the emotional level I'd hoped and intended they would. I'm pleased that someone would publish this songbook of my music and grateful that you who have purchased this book would wish to play my music.

Best wishes,

Will Ackerman
Windham County, VT

THE Will Ackerman COLLECTION

Contents

4	A Note
5	Will Ackerman
8	The Music
10	Windham Hill Recordings by Will Ackerman
11	Anne's Song
15	The Bricklayer's Beautiful Daughter
18	Climbing in Geometry
23	Conferring With the Moon
26	The Impending Death of the Virgin Spirit
37	In a Region of Clouds
32	Passage
30	Processional
42	Shella's Pictures
46	Seattle
52	The Shape of the Land
58	Slow Motion Roast Beef Restaurant Seduction
62	The Townshend Shuffle
72	Visiting

Will Ackerman

"He has had more to do with the rise of acoustic-based instrumental music as a popular form in the '70s and '80s than anyone else."
—www.allmusic.com/

It didn't matter for how many, or for how much. The music came first. After years of performing in elegant concert halls around the world, guitarist Will Ackerman still marvels when he thinks back to Stanford University in the mid-1970s. Now *that* was a time, he recalls, those days of endless, informal jam sessions at any hour, sometimes for only four or five listeners, always playing for free.

"I remember the stairwells, the reverberative spaces we found all over campus," Ackerman says. "The times we sneaked into the chapel and played until dawn. I cut my teeth back then with a lot of other brilliant, if unknown, guitarists like Brooks Yeager and Rich Osborne.

The music came first, like that found on the small Takoma record label. "Takoma was a real eye-opener," Ackerman explains, "showing me there was a genre of acoustic guitar music happening, which added a degree of legitimacy or community to what I was doing. All of us were taking the steel-string guitar out of the realm of purely folk instrument, and establishing a classical discipline for it."

Takoma's masterful trio of guitarists, Robbie Basho, John Fahey, and Leo Kottke influenced Ackerman's developing sound: "I could hear them in there — John's blues; Leo's double-thumbing, dynamic pieces; Robbie's experiments with Indian sitar and, more specifically, sarod music — but I knew that some of it was mine. One of the greatest artistic achievements is to have a unique voice. It seems unlikely that somebody can convey so much of their musical character in only a few notes, but I know it's true."

It was the music, not an on-stage "act" or special costumes. "I remember my first tour, with The

Photo by Bill Reitzel

Persuasions," Ackerman says. "They would change their satin suits between shows, and I changed my flannel shirt." Words of encouragement came from fellow artists like Richie Havens, who believed, as Ackerman says, that "the harmonies of an acoustic stringed instrument will never become obsolete."

Photo by John Cooper

In 1976 he borrowed $300 from friends and started his own acoustic record label, Windham Hill. He really worked as a carpenter, threatening his fingers with power tools, and played guitar on the side. His business card for a while read, "Windham Hill Builders/ Records/ Music (BMI)."

Ackerman started his record company at the height of disco fever, and sold albums in health food stores, but things worked out. Just like when he designed and built his own house, on a hill in Vermont's Windham County, without any blueprints.

The record company grew, a lot, every year, as Windham Hill became the only label with its own section in the music stores, but the pressures grew too. When they wouldn't go away, Ackerman resigned as CEO in 1984. Returning to his property in Vermont, he sometimes worked as a general contractor.

Although he still records for the label, Ackerman sold his remaining interest in Windham Hill in 1992, and passed the three years of a non-compete clause developing a spoken word label, Gang of Seven. He also built a state-of-the-art, state-of-Vermont digital recording studio across the front yard from his house.

In 1996, with former Windham Hill VP and producer Dawn Atkinson, he started a new label, Imaginary Road. Today he is looking to the internet and a new venture.

Ironically, thanks to his tremendous business success and his acclaimed work as a producer, Ackerman's own musical abilities sometimes are overlooked (even by himself). He's a music star who can't read music, who's taken only one lesson, which consisted of Robbie Basho telling him, "You just want the short lesson? Play the guitar on your left knee, and don't be afraid to feel anything." His fans, though, never go away. His tours, no matter how infrequent, sell out.

"People love Will's music for what it is," says Ackerman's long-time associate Virginia Andrew. "He sometimes goes four or five years between releases, and then when a CD appears we get a flood of mail saying, 'Please don't wait so long next time.'"

It always comes back to the music.

Will Ackerman picks up a guitar and begins, in his words, "hunting around. I'm forcing myself to be an explorer. Every single song I do — with one exception — is in a different tuning. I create an absolutely barren landscape for myself by going into a tuning that I don't know. I take the tuning down to nothing, to where the strings are flapping in the breeze, and then bring the sound back up."

"By removing my intellect entirely from the process, I'm staying away from preconceptions, which forces me to find the structure of the tuning — to find the melodic lines, the harmonic lines. And then I begin to construct."

"I don't have a melody in my mind. I keep running at it, letting my fingers find it. I play the same thing over and over again, I keep going back to the beginning, and wait to see what's going to emerge. The intellect only becomes involved after I have two or three sections of a song that I need to bridge."

This process has worked its magic for almost three decades. "As I get older, I feel more freedom," Ackerman says. "One of the joys is that I don't feel the music has become old hat to me. The mystery and the discovery is no less than it ever was, and I'm enjoying performing now more than I ever have."

The simplicity of his music, the guitarist says, leaves "nothing to hide behind." Every note has the potential to be interpreted, is potentially meaningful. "These days," he says, "I feel like I'm revisiting these songs and finding a subtlety in them that I didn't know was there."

Photo by Bill Reitzel

The best of Will Ackerman's music is presented here for you to enjoy (and yes, admire). "I'm very proud of these examples of what I've done," he says. The music will continue, too, for he's currently recording his eleventh CD.

As for his future?

"People keep asking me for some kind of mission statement," Ackerman says, "and I keep not delivering it. I am what I am. I haven't evolved. This is what I do, and you either like it or you don't. What I'm about is a ballad structure, melody, harmony, and an emotional connection."

—**Richard Sassaman, May 1999**

THE MUSIC

ANNE'S SONG

I was very proud when Robbie Basho told me that he felt this was my best piece. It combines the trademark sound of the intro with some of the more challenging guitar playing I've ever accomplished. I normally allow myself to be very comfortable in what I write, being content to play what comes naturally. I actually forced myself into ideas and performance on this piece which were somewhat beyond the natural or comfortable place for me. I think this is the only piece currently in my songlist where the tuning is also used on another song, that being "Hawk Circle."

BRICKLAYER'S BEAUTIFUL DAUGHTER

This song simply appeared note-for-note one day, literally within an hour; I'll always be grateful for the gift of it and consider it my best piece, if that's not too immodest to say. It was written in a time where the sort of classicism at work in "Processional" still guided me and so it has a more traditional song and harmonic structure than much of my later work. Like "Processional," I still play this in concert and have found it to lend itself to a wide range of interpretations, most notably in volume dynamics.

CLIMBING IN GEOMETRY

Another song written in a tempo to keep things from getting too soporific. The first piece I ever wrote which I think clearly reflects my love of Alex deGrassi's music was Remedios (The Beauty) and this is another of those pieces which would not have existed without Alex's innovation.

CONFERRING WITH THE MOON

A bit too much red wine and way too much moonlight. An out loud talk with La Luna about love, which was not going at all well. The piece, while not an imitation of Alex deGrassi by any means, utilizes a fluid picking style that could not have come about in me were it not for Alex's pieces like "Turning: Turning Back."

IMPENDING DEATH OF THE VIRGIN SPIRIT

My mother died when I was 12. It was an immediate and wrenching birth from childhood innocence to an awareness of the world's pain. I wrote this piece to try to recapture the quiescence and innocence just before her death, but was not able to remove the sadness of what I knew was just moments in the future. This piece doesn't remind me much of any guitar influences and I think of it as one of the earliest pieces in which I sensed I might have a "voice" musically.

IN A REGION OF CLOUDS

A typically moody piece which definitely offers some sunlight as well. I've always thought this could work well as a setting for a guitar duet, but have never actually performed it in this way.

PASSAGE

The song is about all the doors we walk through, or are pushed through, in life. It reminds me both structurally and emotionally of an earlier piece I wrote entitled "It Takes A Year." I think of this one as being a piece which sounds very obviously like my writing.

PROCESSIONAL

This was written for a theater production of Romeo and Juliet; literally a processional in which the actors took the stage. It was meant to convey a classicism in structure and a foreshadowing of the emotional content of the play. I still play this piece in concert and manage to find new interpretations of it after playing it for twenty-some years. A lot can be done with both volume and tempo dynamics on this piece.

SEATTLE

A double-thumbing piece which follows "The Rediscovery of Big Bug Creek, Arizona" and "The Townshend Shuffle" chronologically and reveals more of my own character than those earlier pieces. "The Townshend Shuffle" seems to me to be just an up-tempo banjo song, "Rediscovery" seems like a sped-up version of a John Fahey composition, but "Seattle" is maybe a little bit more mature and my own — though I doubt it would have existed without Leo Kottke.

THE SHAPE OF THE LAND

A song about the Vermont countryside after the leaves fall and the shape of the land, which is for the summer hidden in dense green leaves, is revealed.

SHELLA'S PICTURES

I was looking at a box of Shella's childhood pictures and was struck by all the smiling faces of parents and children and friends at birthdays, Christmases, and Halloweens. What struck me was not the smiles themselves, but the knowledge that behind and below these smiles there is always sadness. I like this piece as much as anything I've written and I have added it to my concert list.

SLOW MOTION ROAST BEEF RESTAURANT SEDUCTION

I think this was the first piece that sounded like me, or where I first stopped imitating John Fahey, Robbie Basho, and Leo Kottke.

TOWNSHEND SHUFFLE

Really nothing more than a guitar rendition of a traditional-sounding banjo piece. It was written probably to keep people awake in concert. The music closest to my heart are the slow ballads, but an entire evening of ballads would probably put me to sleep as well.

VISITING

A free-flowing chordal piece that was always meant to have a melodic line in addition to the guitar part. That melody was supplied in the recording by Chuck Greenberg of Shadowfax who, sadly, passed away a few years ago. I used to perform it with Chuck in concert, but have, in memory of him, begun to perform it solo in concert. I was surprised to find that, in using a fairly heavy dose of chorusing, that the piece actually works quite well as a solo.

WINDHAM HILL RECORDINGS BY WILL ACKERMAN

In Search of the Turtle's Navel, 1976

It Takes a Year, 1977

Childhood and Memory, 1979

Passage, 1981

Past Light, 1983

Conferring With the Moon, 1986

Imaginary Road, 1988

The Opening of Doors, 1992

Retrospective, 1993

Sound of Wind Driven Rain, 1998

Photo by John Cooper

Anne's Song

By William Ackerman

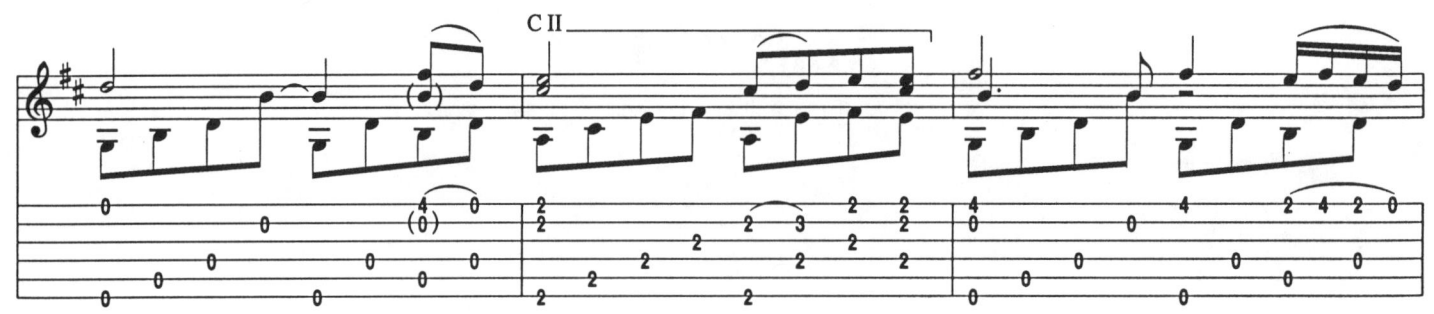
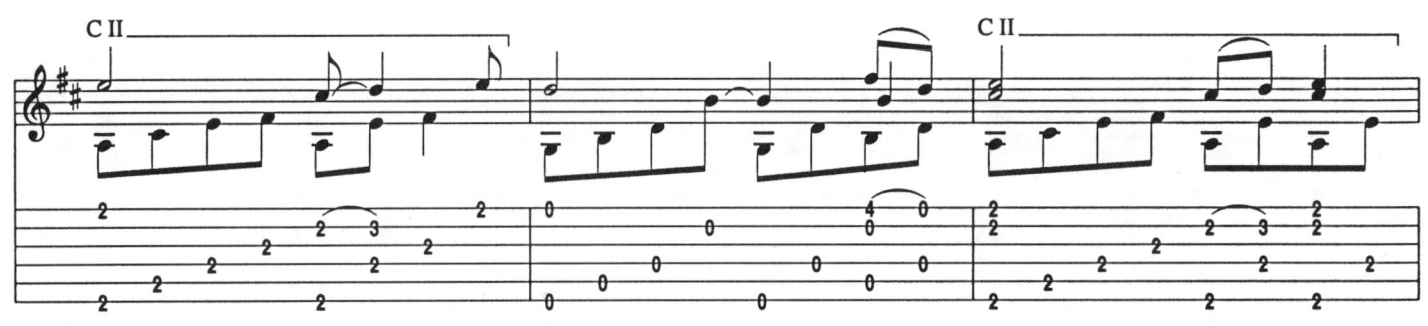
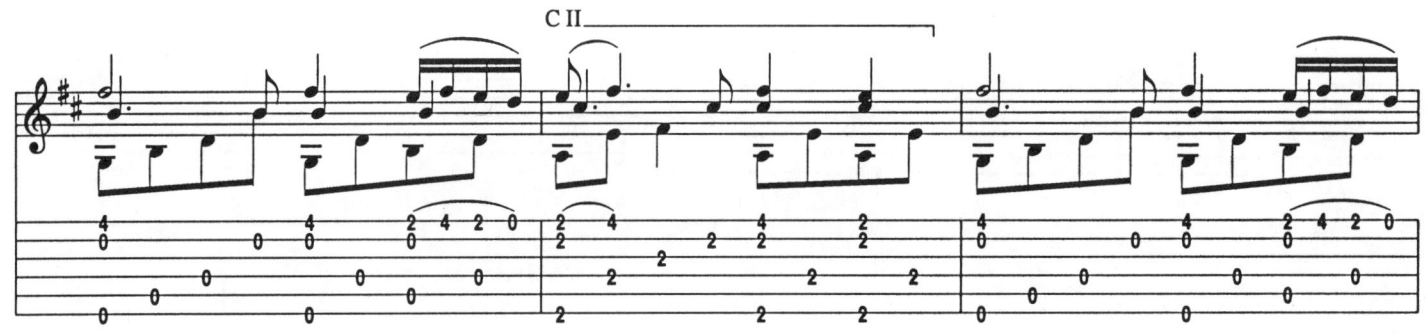
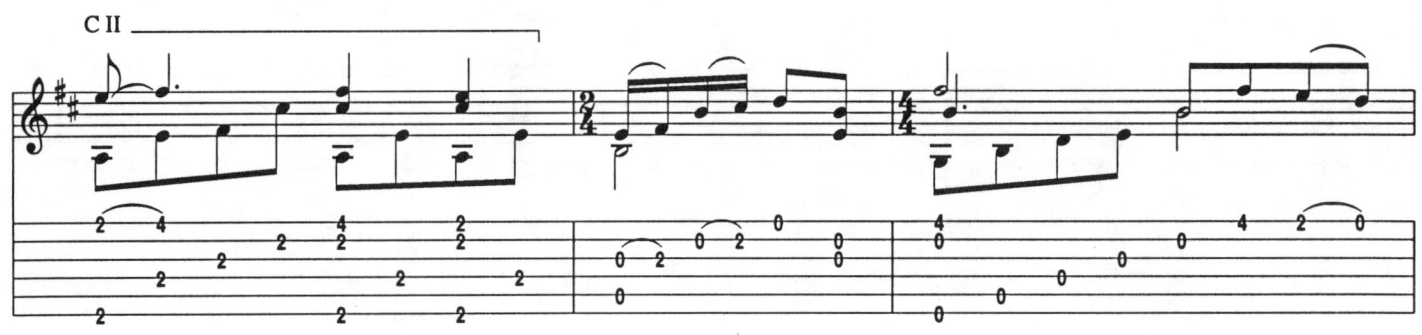
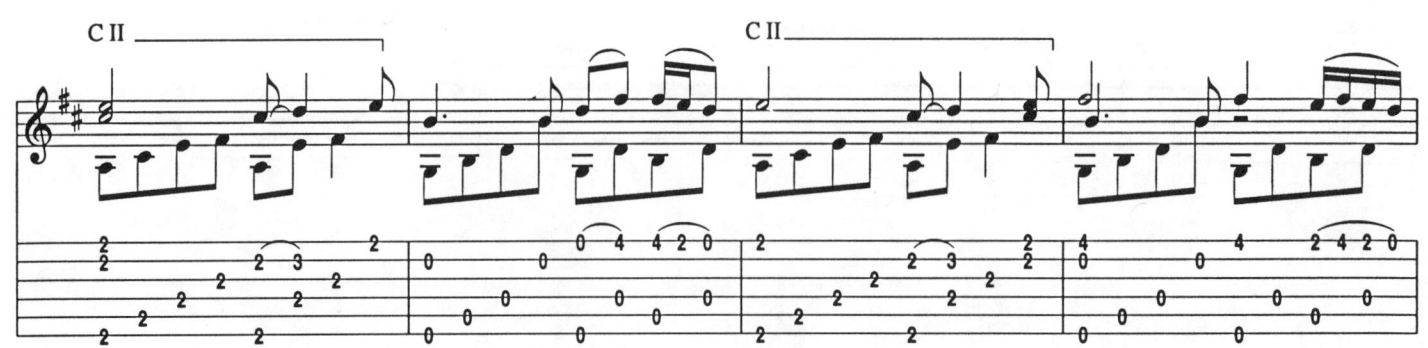

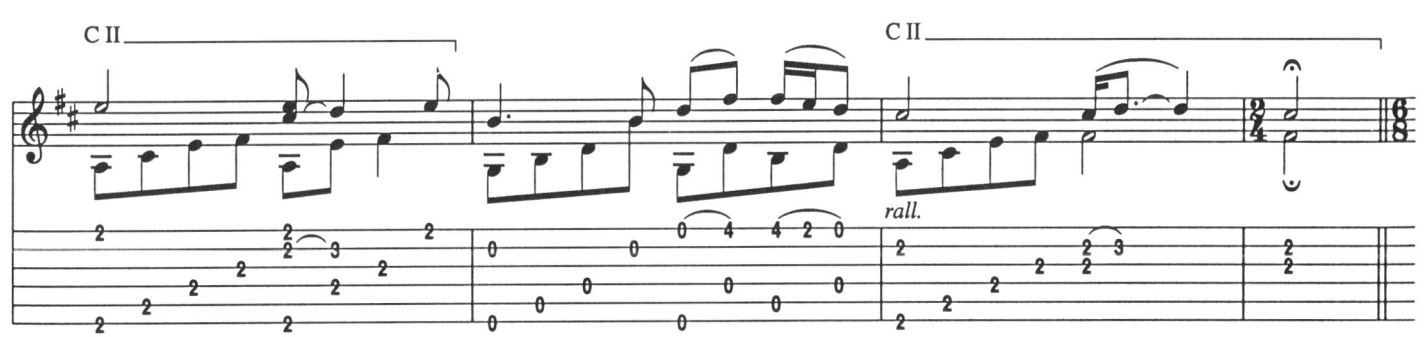

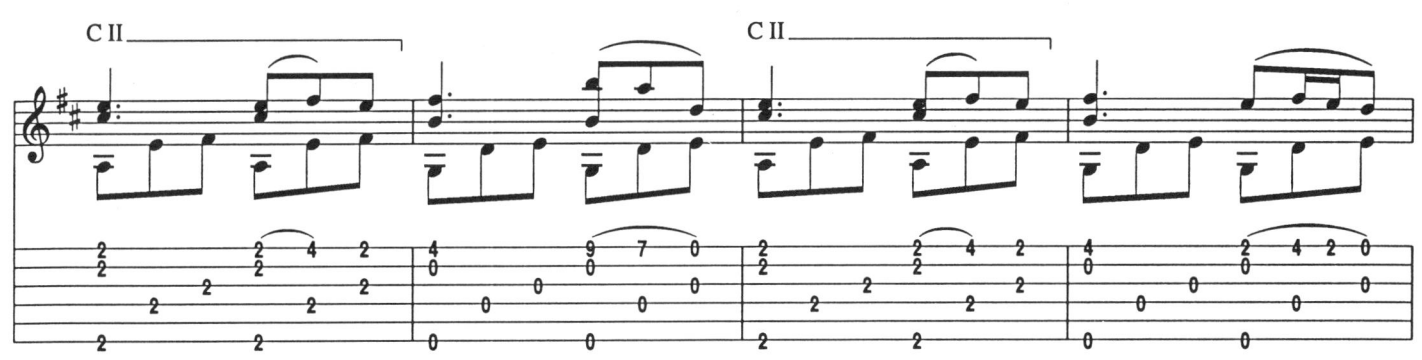

13

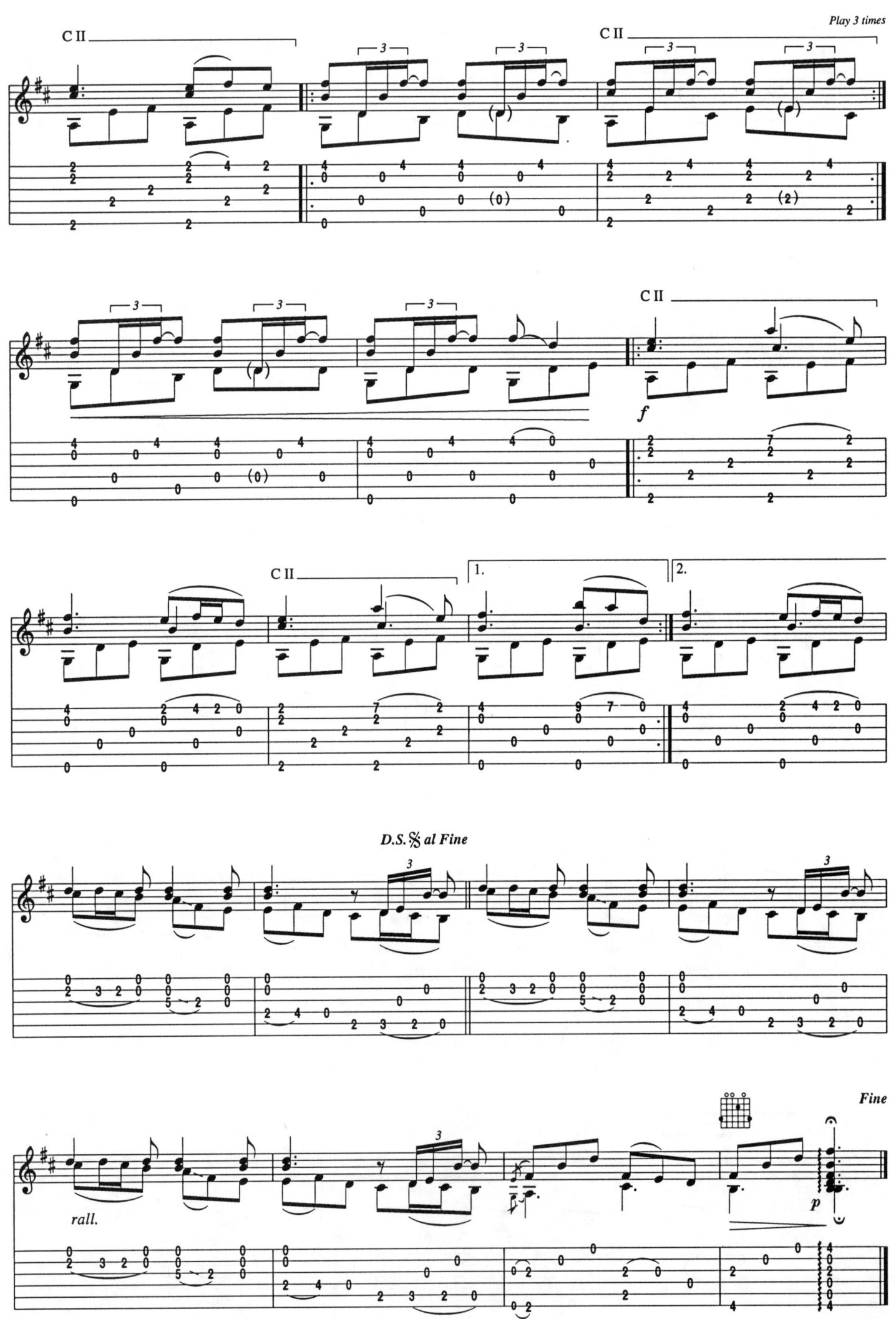

The Bricklayer's Beautiful Daughter

By William Ackerman

Copyright © 1977 Imaginary Road Music (BMI)
All Rights Reserved   Used by Permission

(Chorus/Double effects ends)

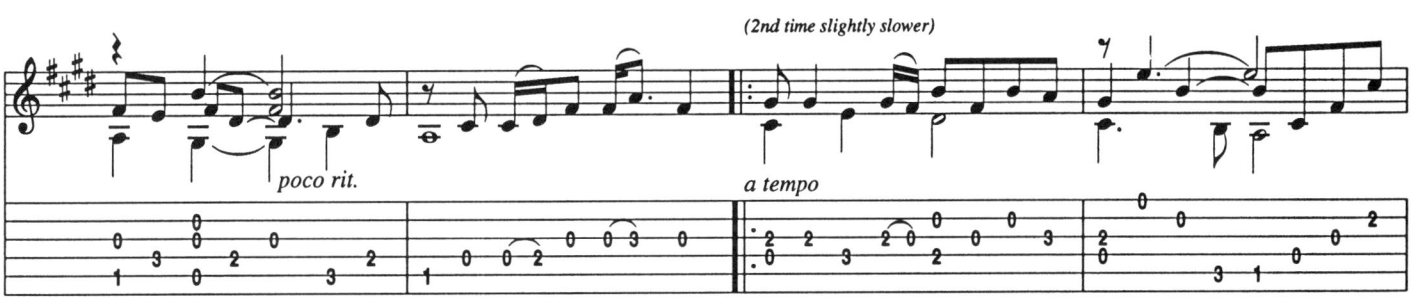

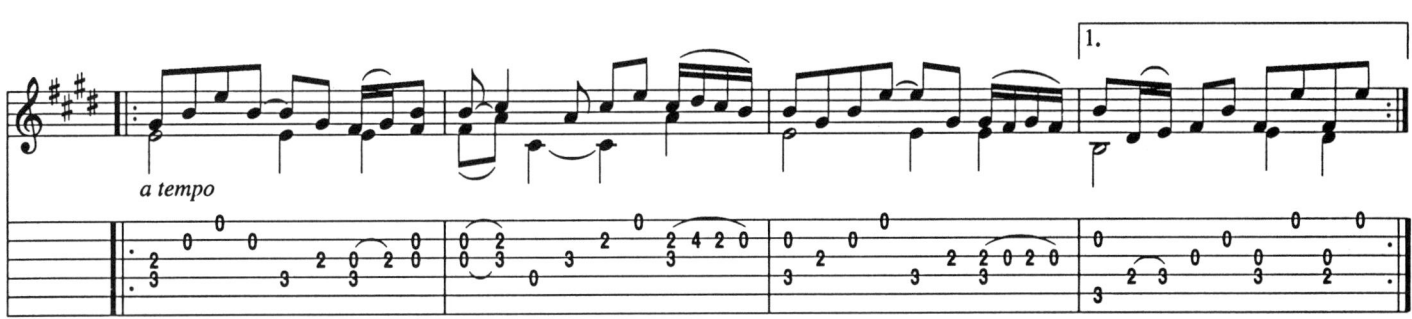

17

Climbing in Geometry

By William Ackerman

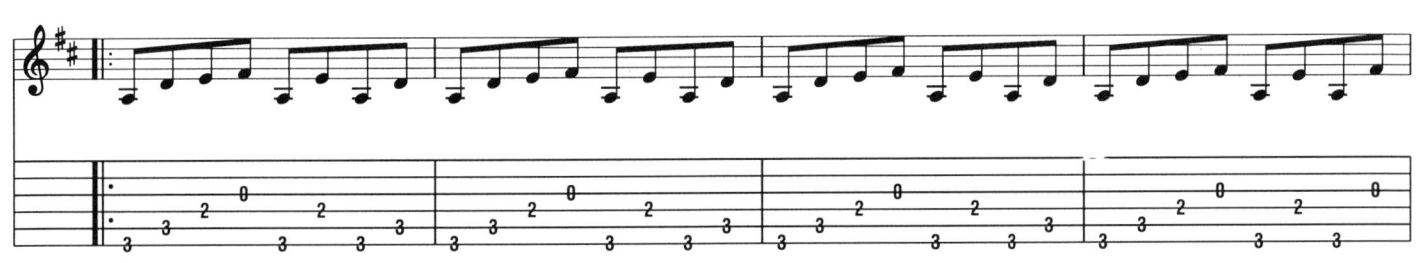

Conferring With the Moon
By William Ackerman

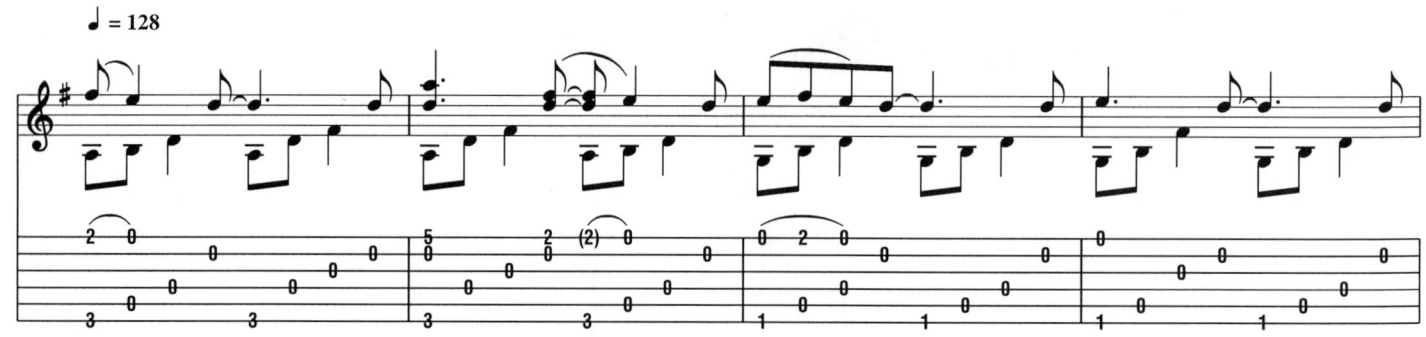

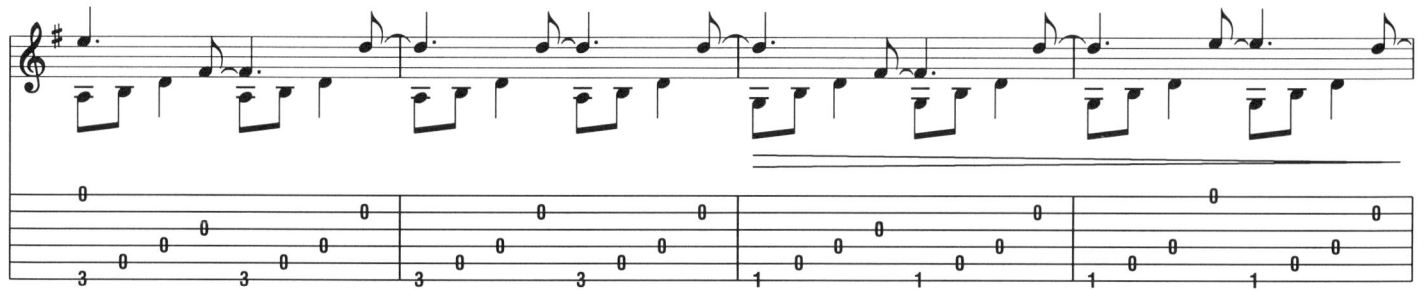

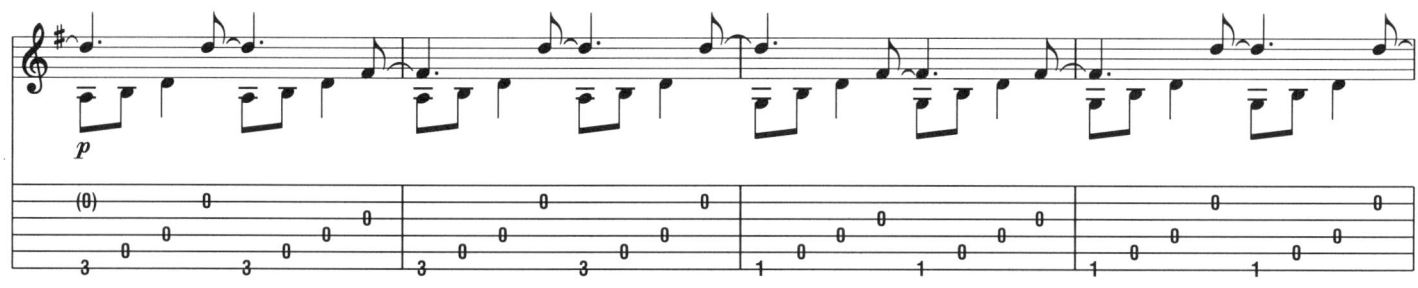

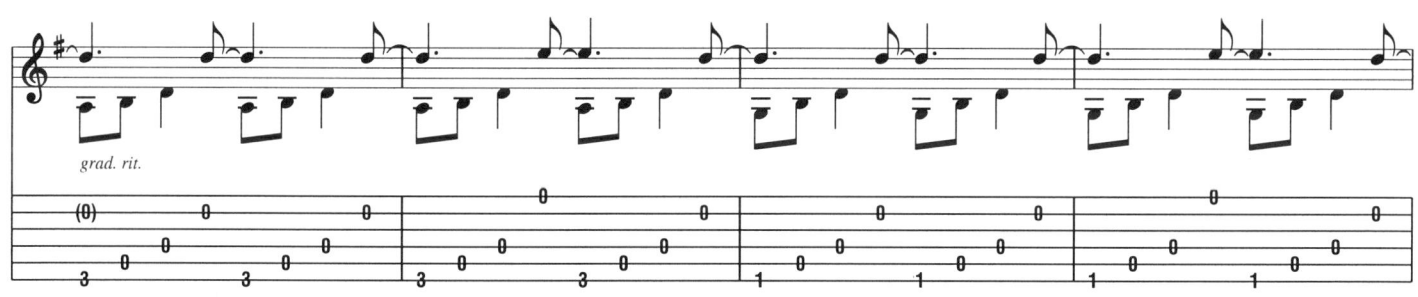

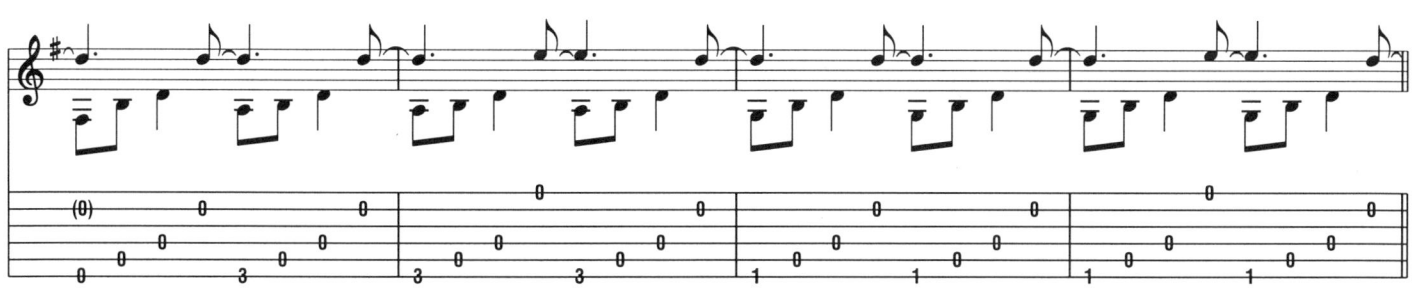

Play 4 Times and Fade

25

The Impending Death of the Virgin Spirit

By William Ackerman

Tuning, Capo II:
①= E ④= C#
②= A ⑤= A
③= G# ⑥= C#

Copyright © 1977 Imaginary Road Music (BMI)
All Rights Reserved   Used by Permission

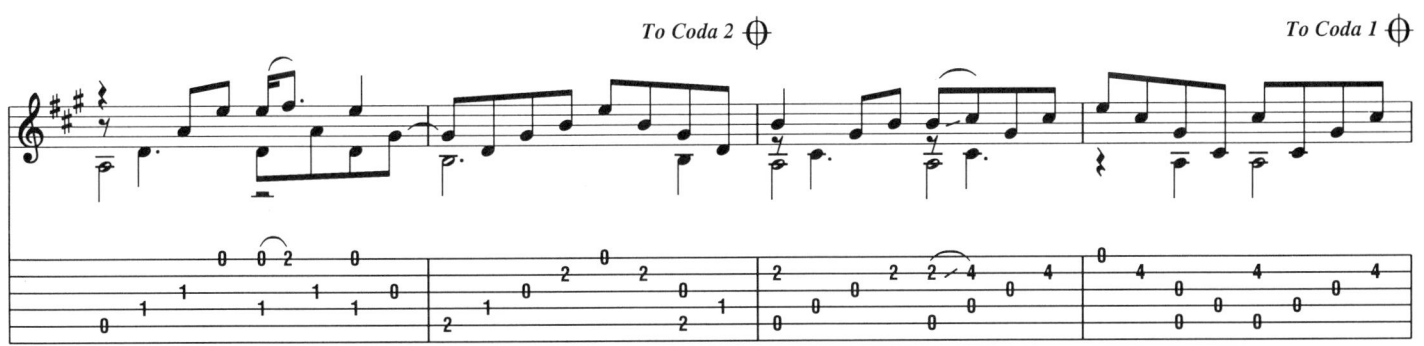
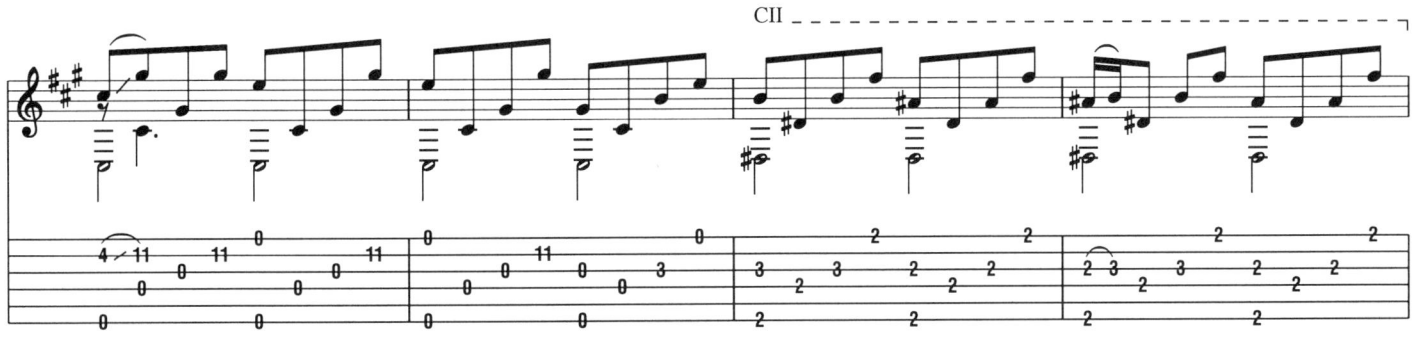
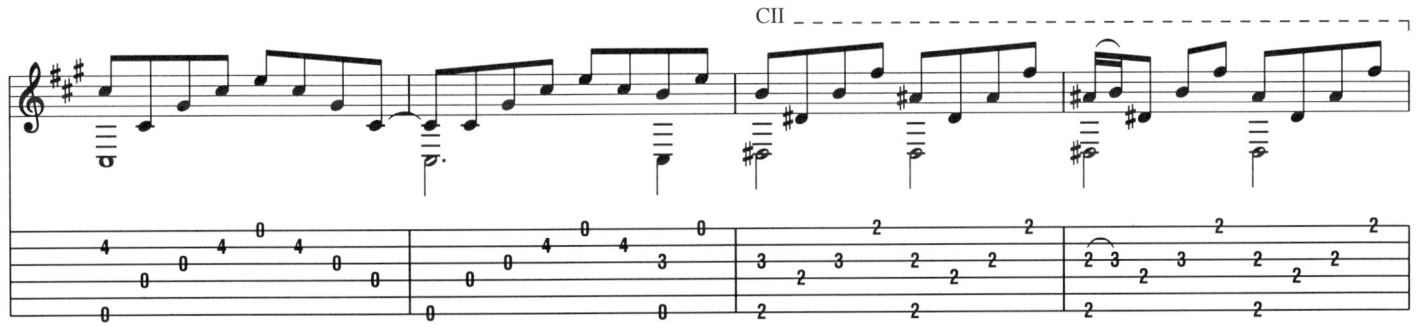
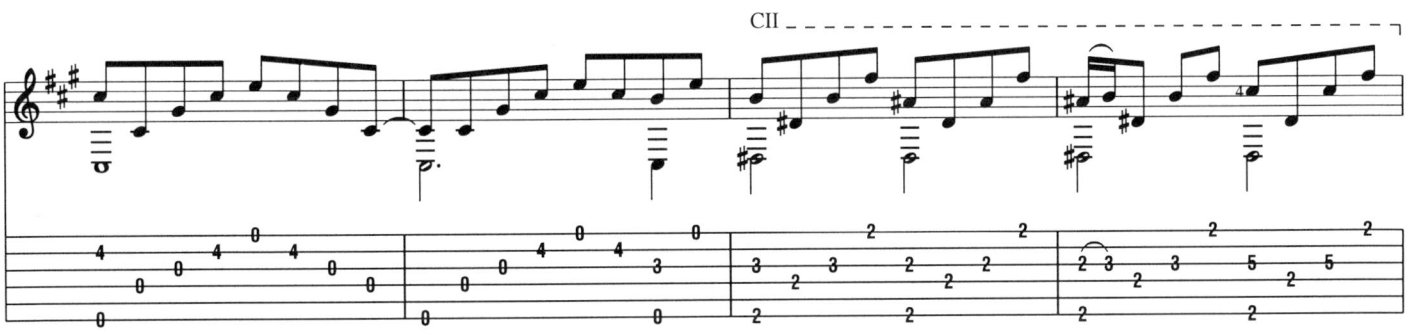

* slight pause

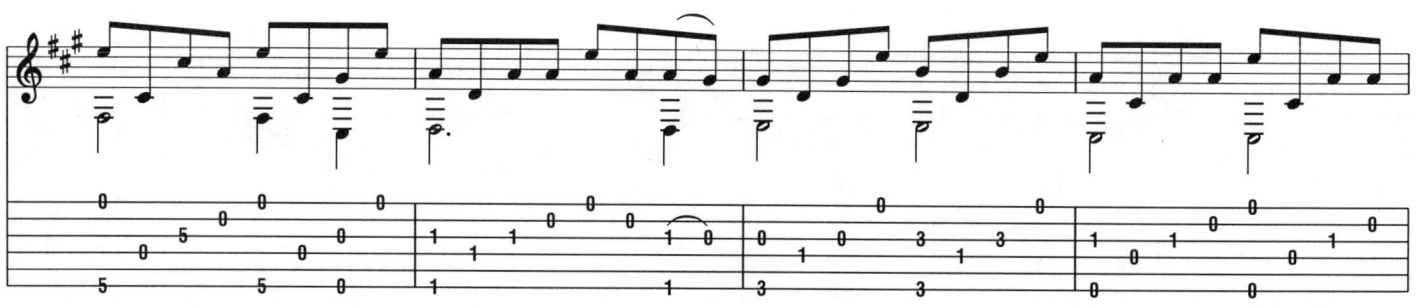

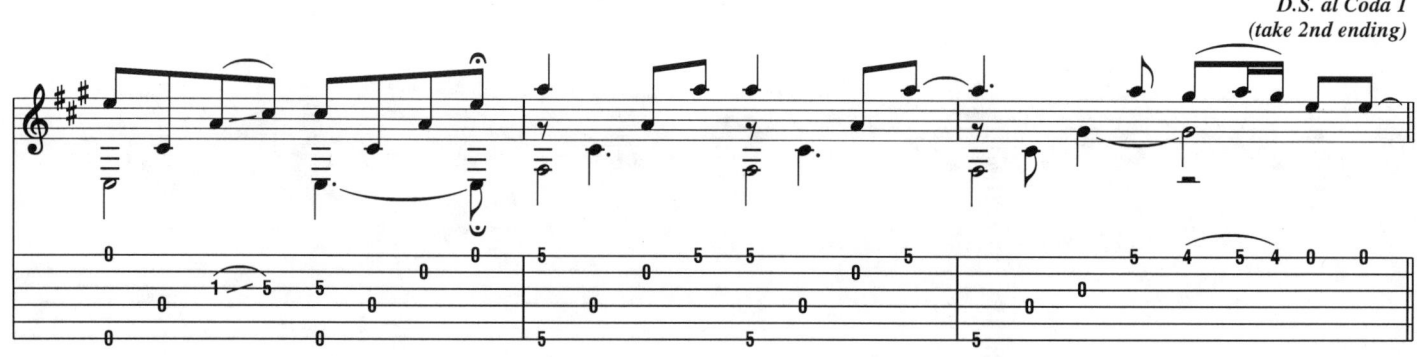

*D.S. al Coda 1
(take 2nd ending)*

⊕ Coda 1

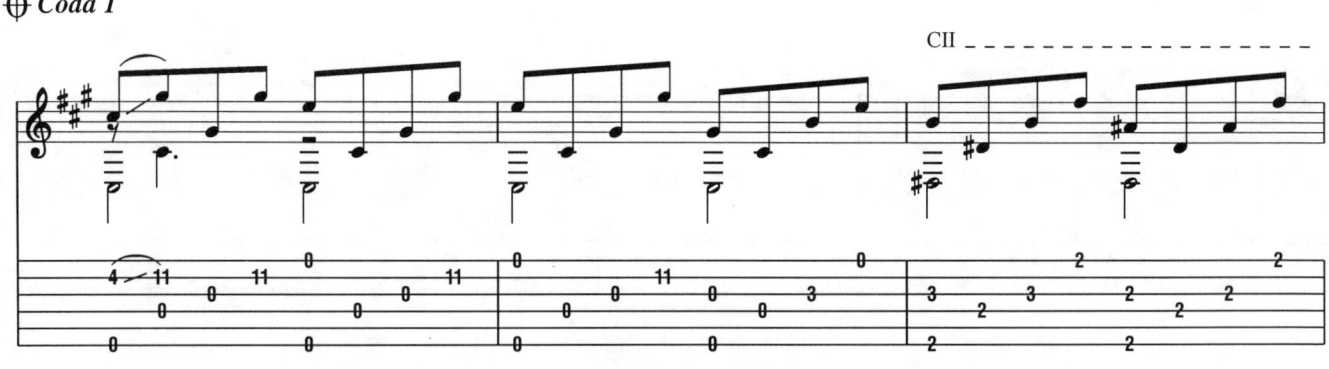

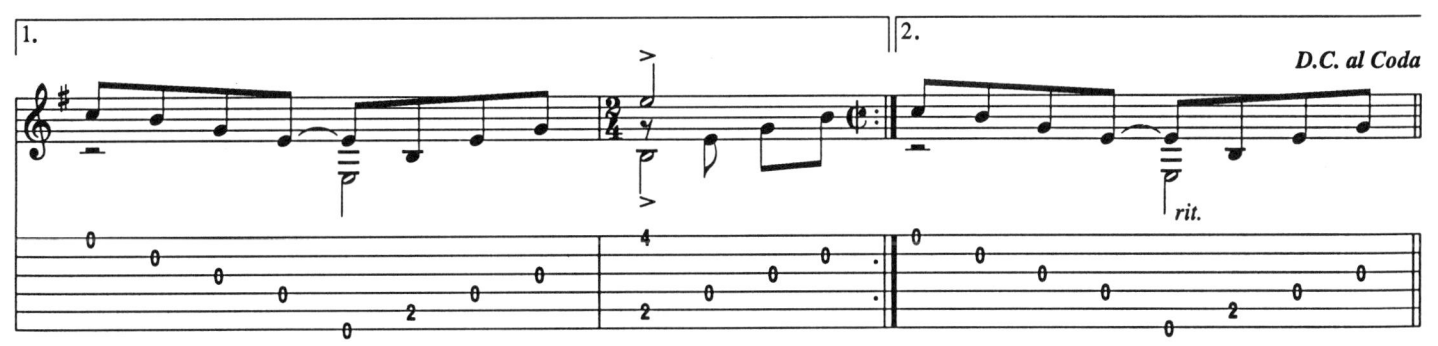

Passage

By William Ackerman

Copyright © 1981 Imaginary Road Music (BMI)
All Rights Reserved   Used by Permission

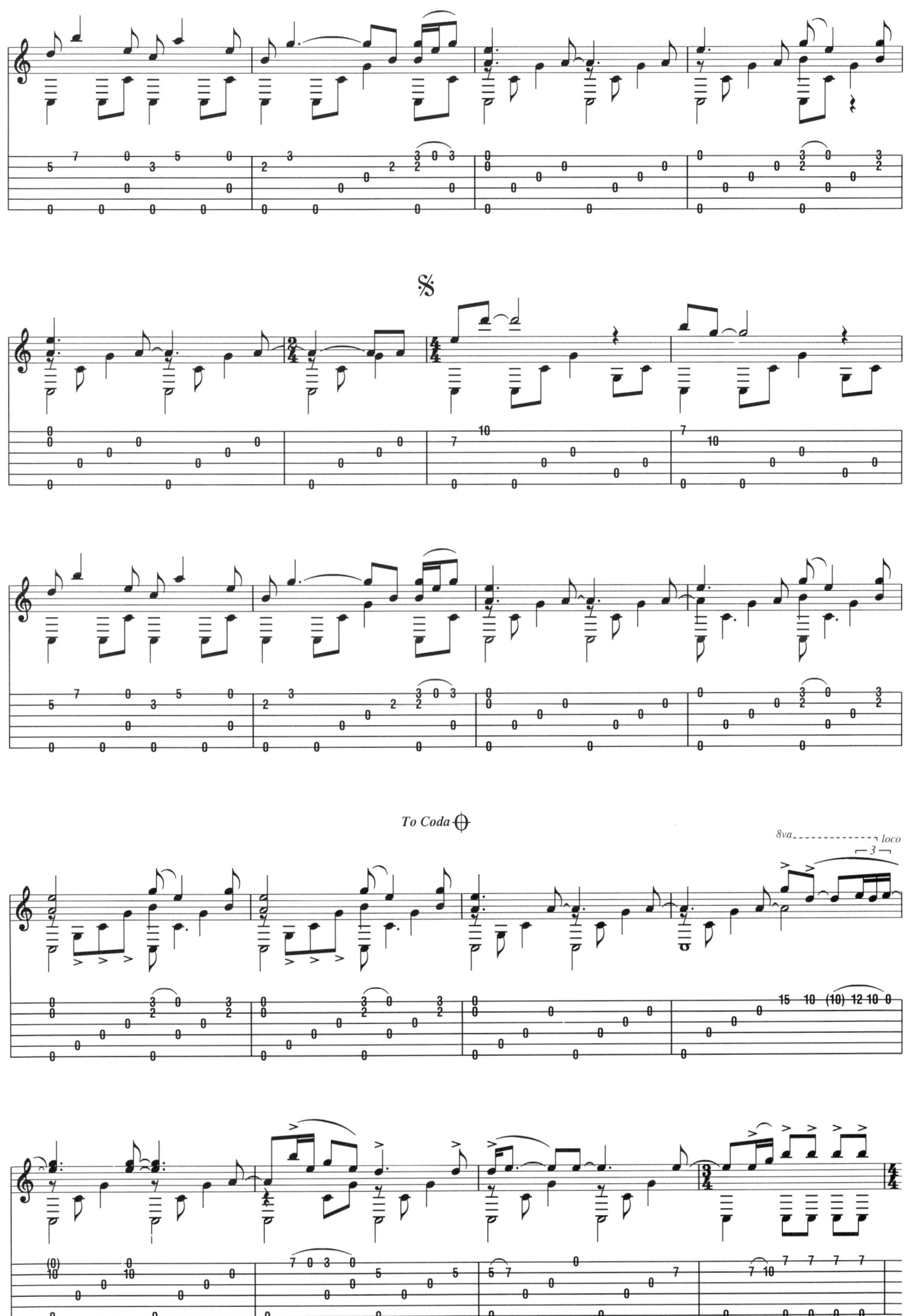

33

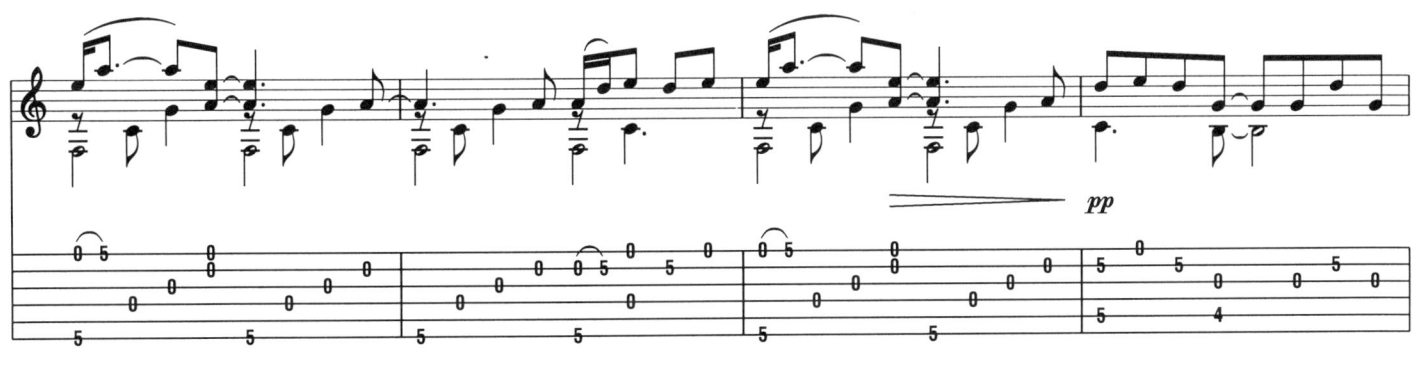

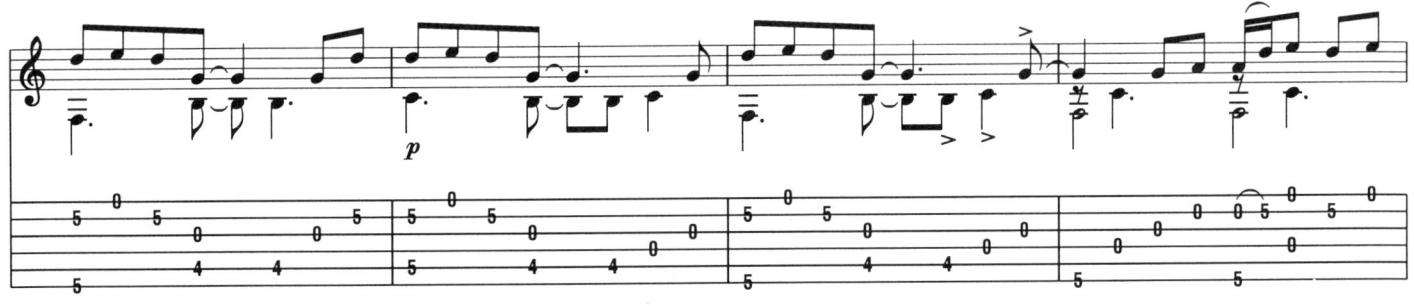

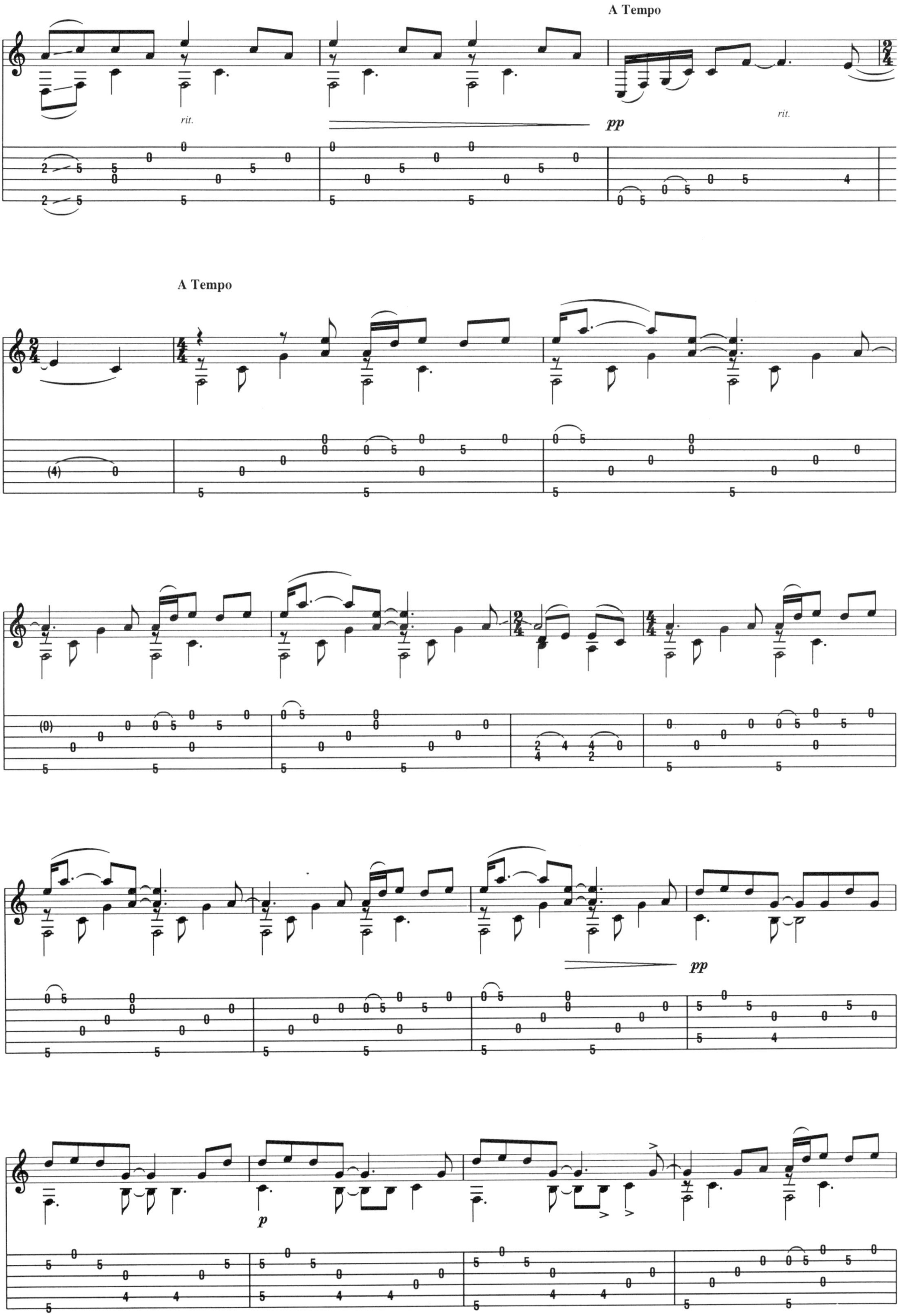
A Tempo
rit.
pp
rit.
A Tempo
pp
p

In a Region of Clouds

By William Ackerman

Tuning:
① = D ④ = B
② = A ⑤ = G
③ = G ⑥ = E

poco rit.

D.C. al Coda

Coda

cresc.   *poco cresc.*

poco cresc.   *poco cresc.*

39

41

Shella's Pictures

By William Ackerman

Tuning:
① = D# ④ = D#
② = B   ⑤ = C#
③ = A# ⑥ = F#

Seattle

By William Ackerman

Capo 3rd fret
Tuning:
① = D   ④ = D
② = A   ⑤ = A
③ = D   ⑥ = D

Moderately fast (♩ = 128-135)

f let ring throughout

* drag index finger back   * drag index finger back

Copyright © 1979 Imaginary Road Music (BMI)
All Rights Reserved   Used by Permission

* drag index finger back

No repeat on D.S. al Coda I

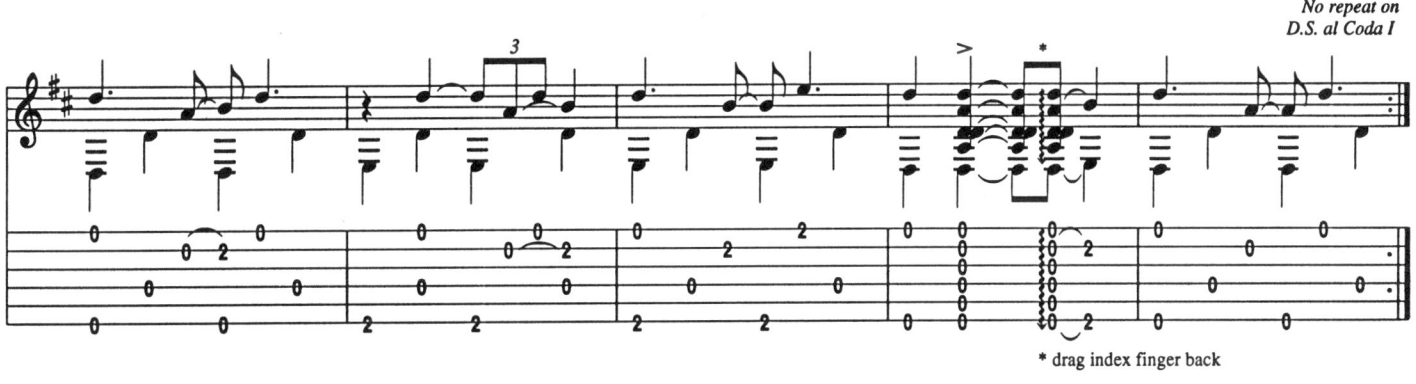

* drag index finger back

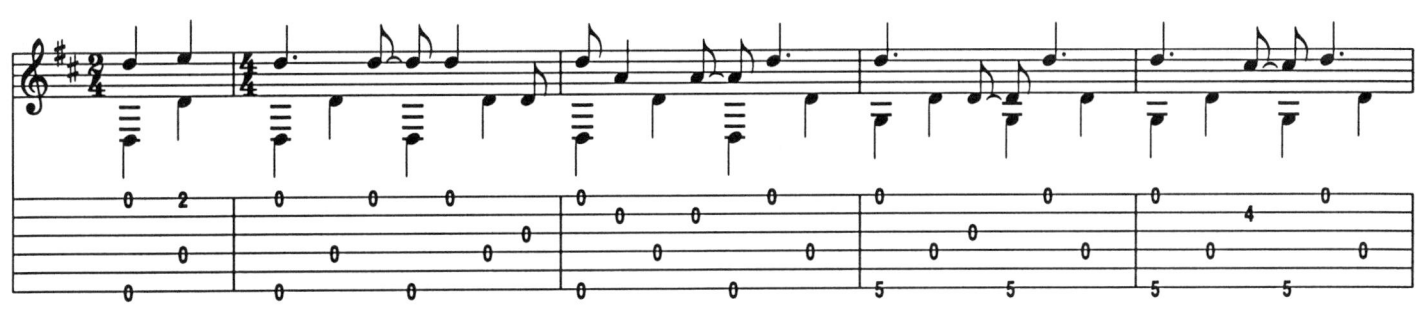

D.S. 𝄋 al Coda I

* drag index finger back

◯ Coda I

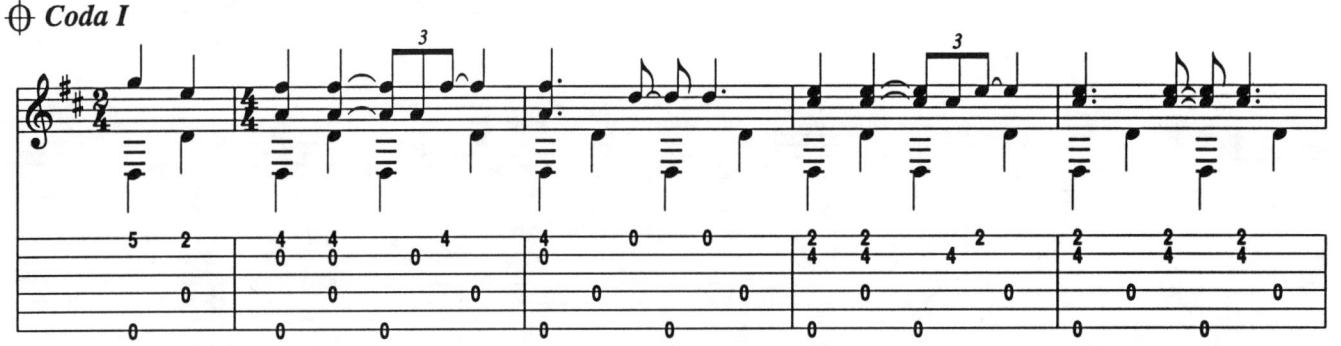

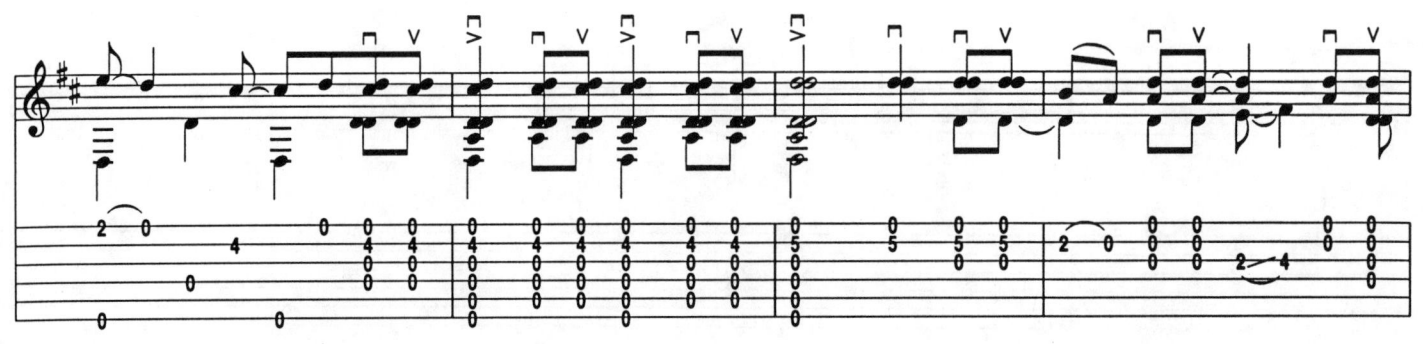

* drag index finger back

The Shape of the Land

By William Ackerman

Tuning, Capo V:
① = D   ④ = C
② = C   ⑤ = B♭
③ = F   ⑥ = E♭

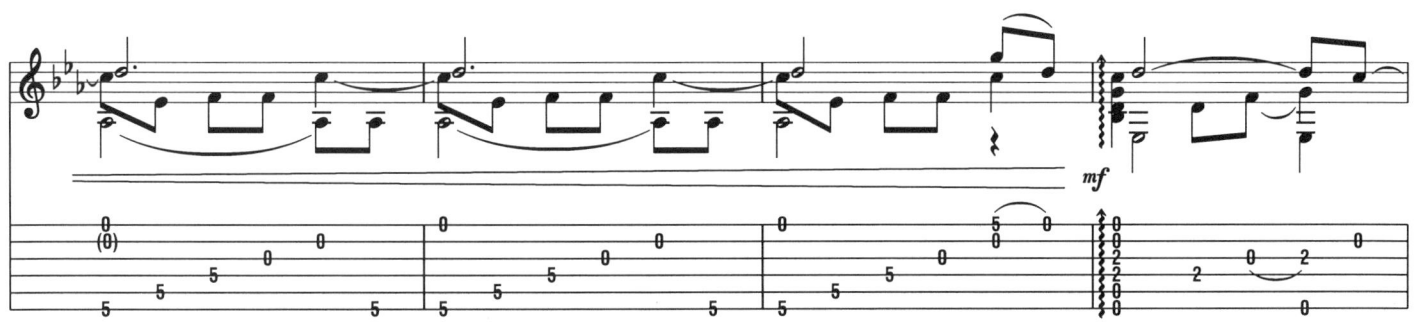

53

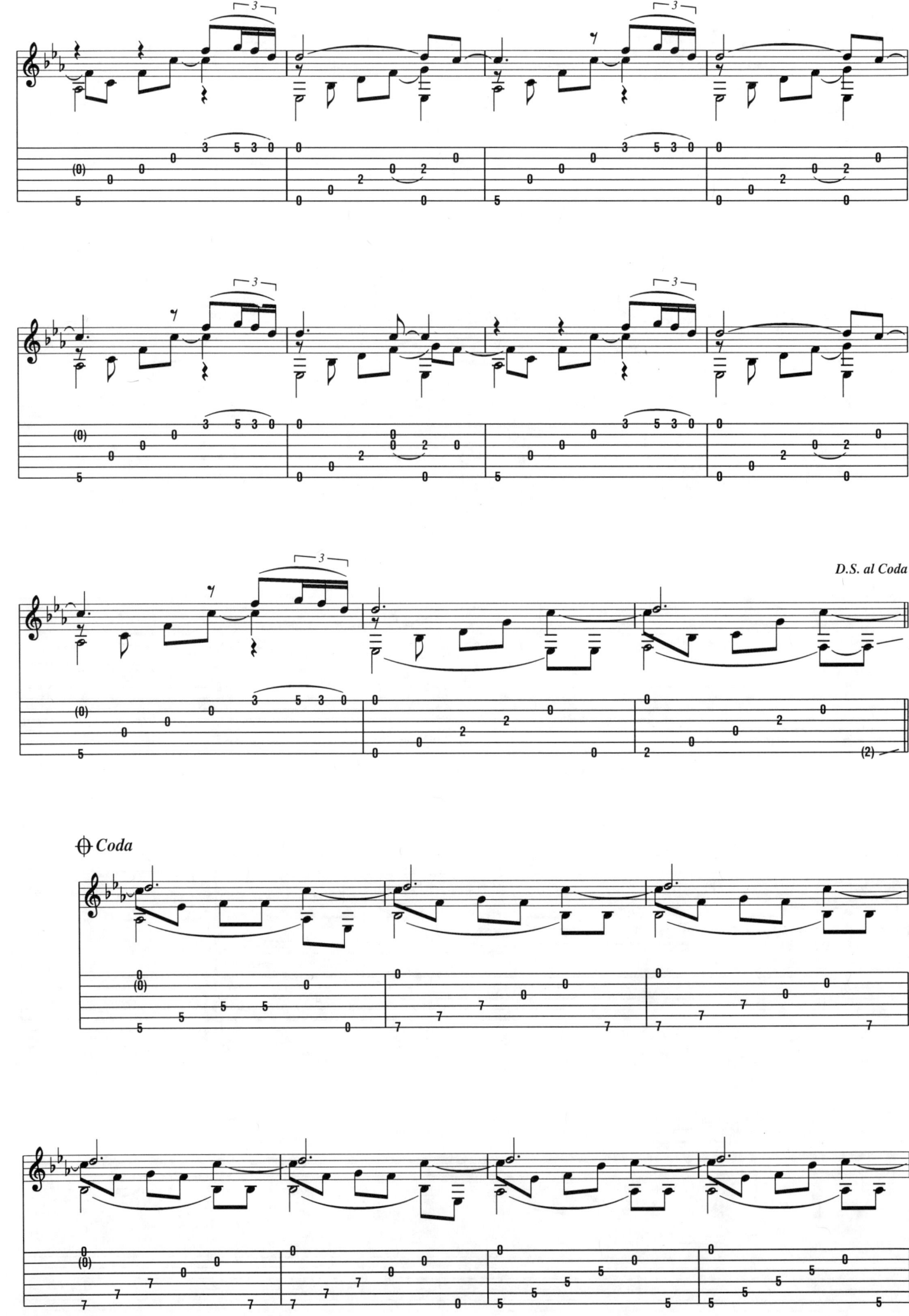

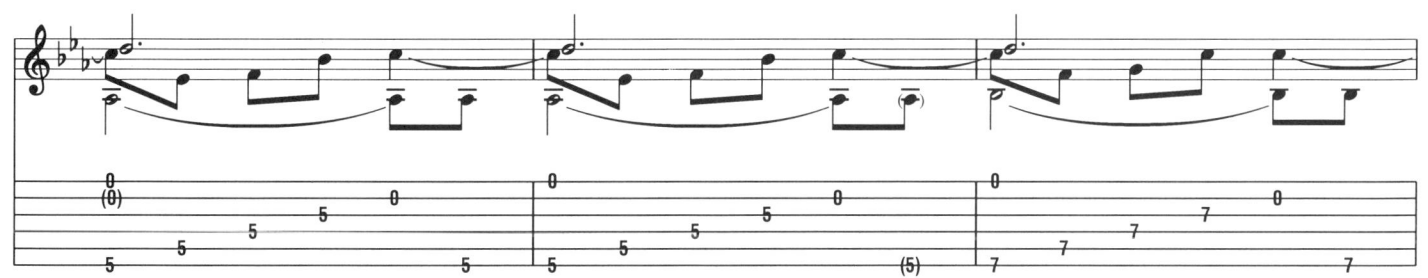

Slow Motion Roast Beef Restaurant Seduction

By William Ackerman

Tuning, Capo II:
① = C# ④ = C#
② = B   ⑤ = F#
③ = E   ⑥ = E

Freely ♩ = 95

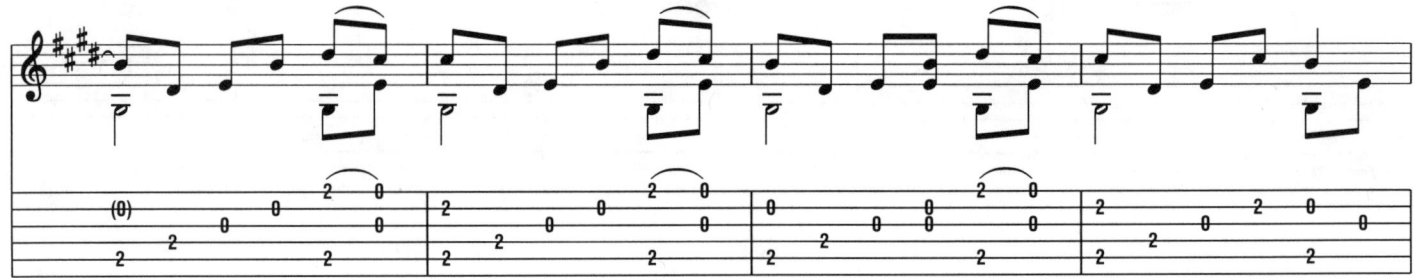

Copyright © 1976 Imaginary Road Music (BMI)
All Rights Reserved   Used by Permission

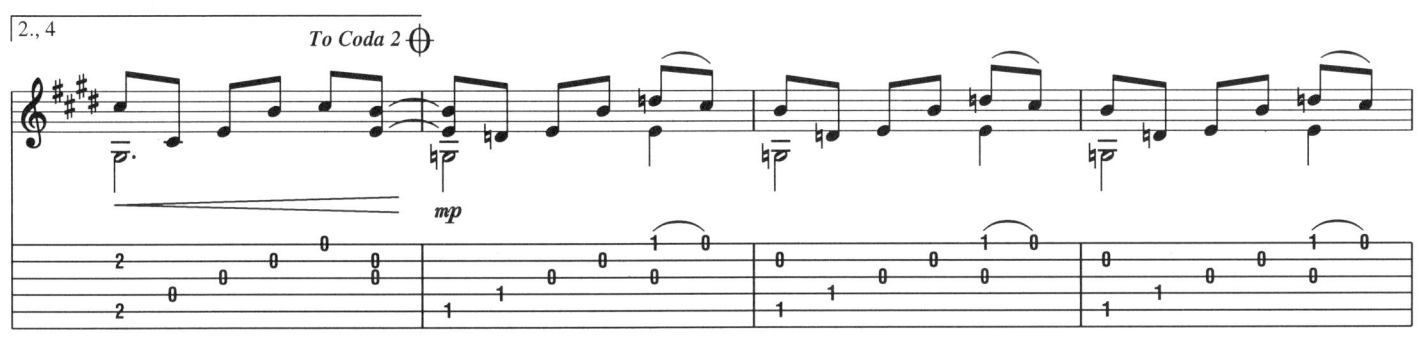

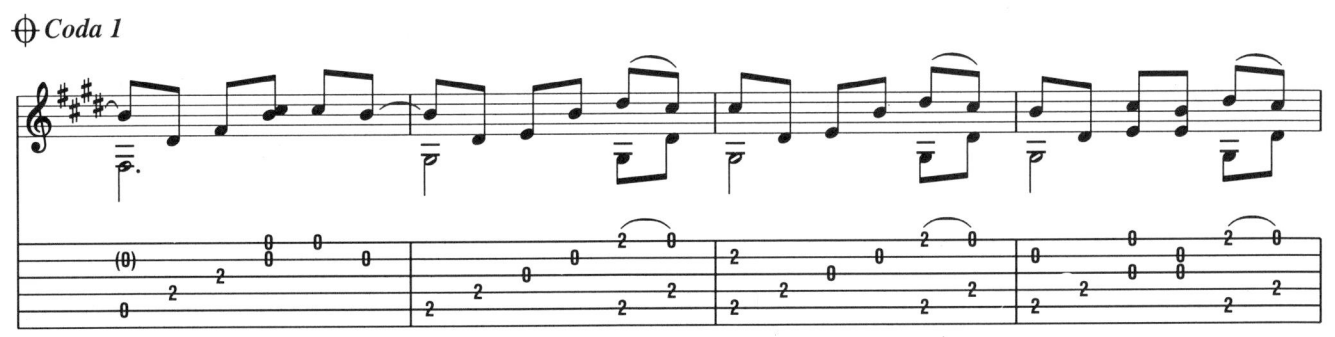

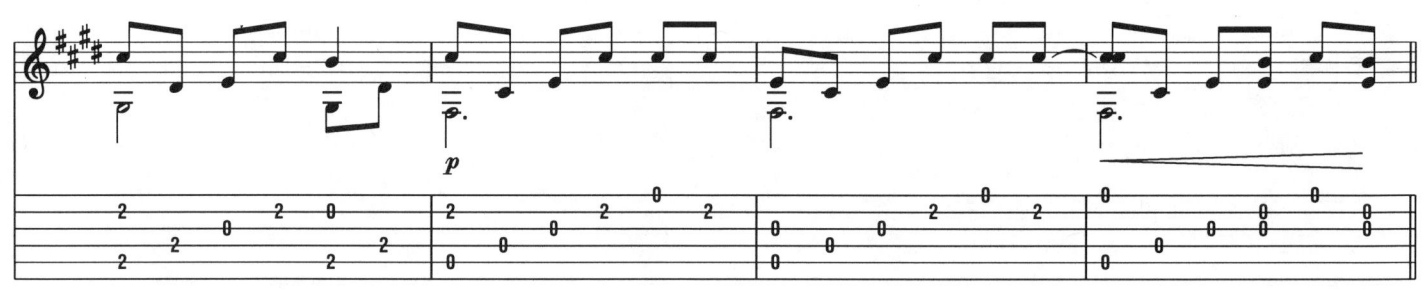

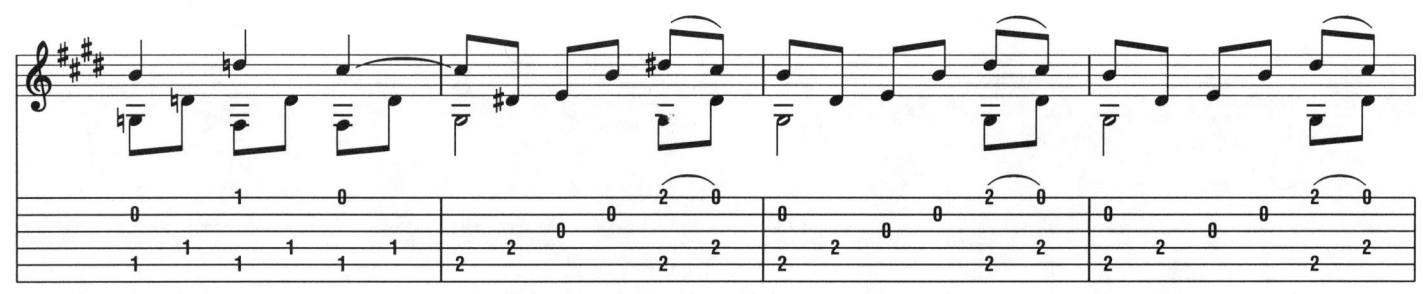

*Brush with thumb, drag back index finger

61

The Townshend Shuffle

By William Ackerman

Copyright © 1977 Imaginary Road Music (BMI)
All Rights Reserved   Used by Permission

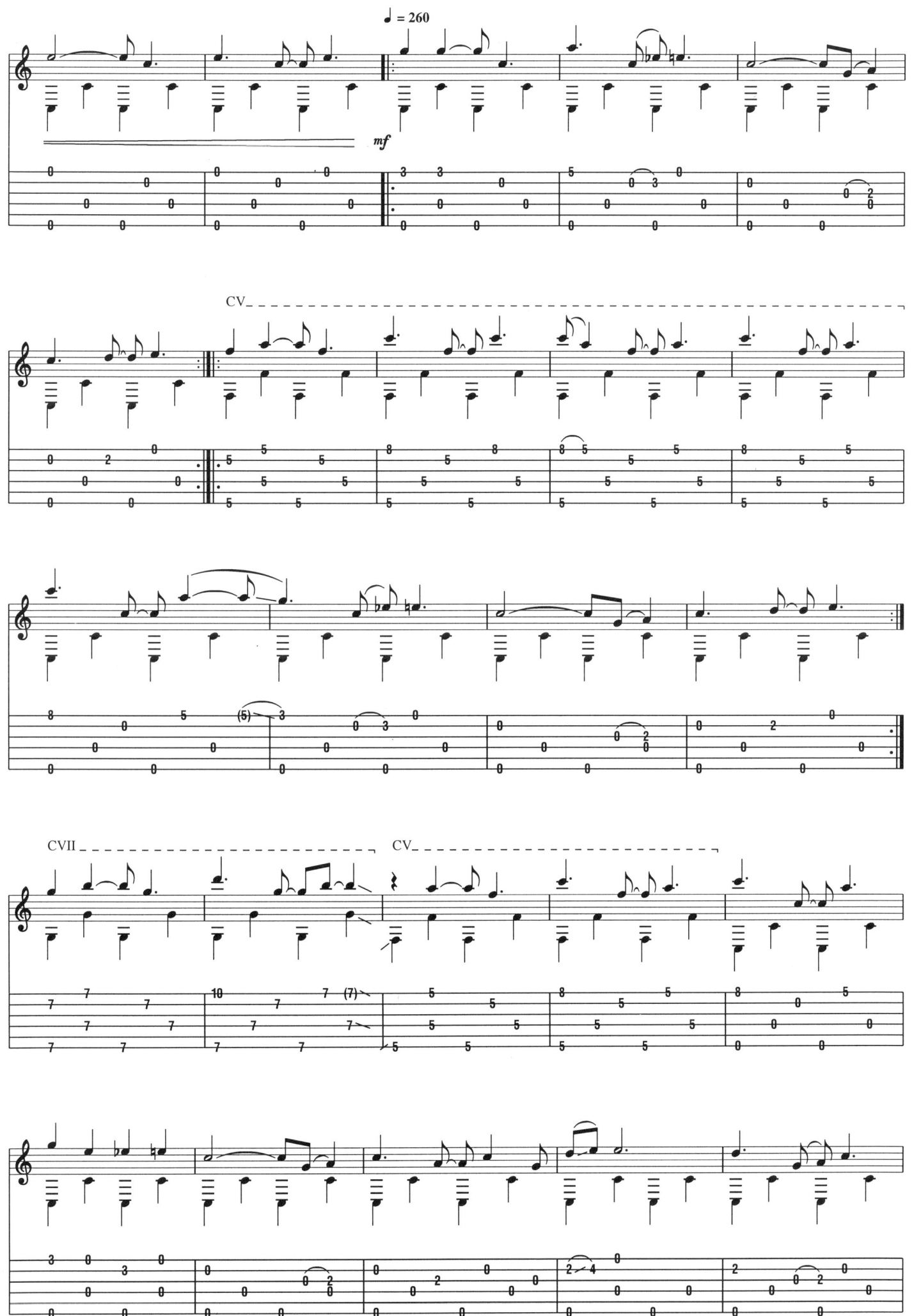

69

Visiting

By William Ackerman

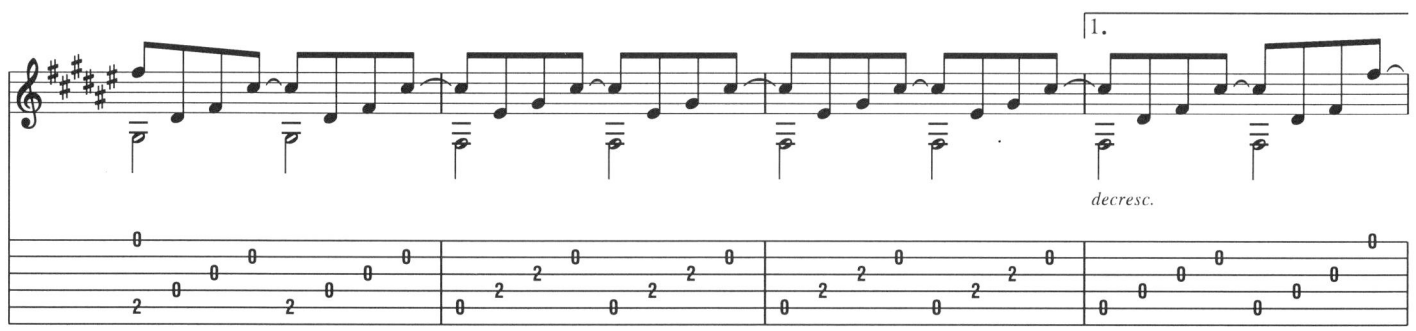

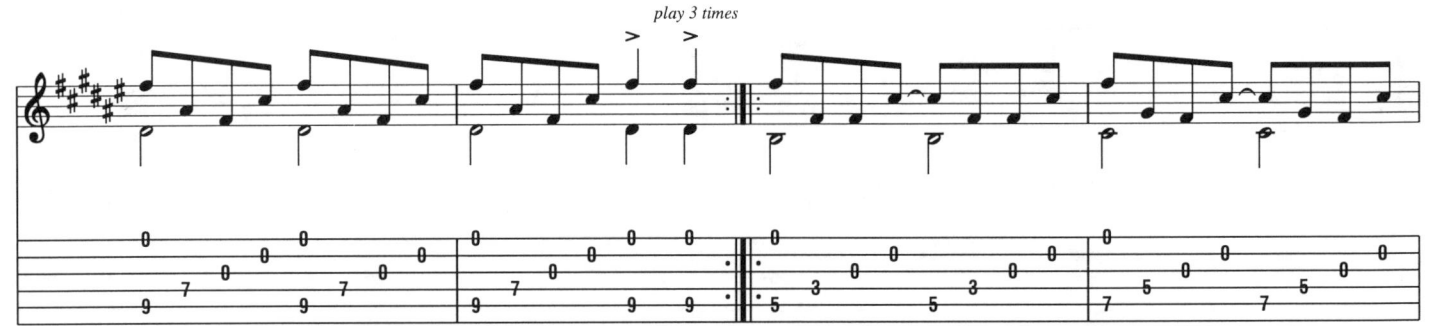

More Fingerstyle Favorites
from Hal•Leonard

12 Wedding Songs
arranged for medium voice and fingerstyle guitar
The collection combines classical/traditional and popular selections. The guitar part is presented in both standard notation and tablature. Contents: Annie's Song • Ave Maria (Shubert) • The First Time I Saw Your Face • Here, There And Everywhere • I Swear • If • In My Life • Jesu, Joy Of Man's Desiring • Let It Be Me • Unchained Melody • When I Fall In Love • You Needed Me.
00740007.................................$12.95

American Folk Songs For Fingerstyle Guitar
25 songs, including: Amazing Grace • America The Beautiful • Home On The Range • I've Been Working On The Railroad • My Old Kentucky Home • When Johnny Comes Marching Home • and more.
00698981.................................$12.95

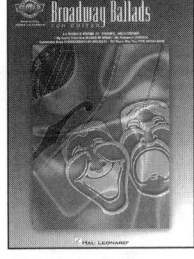

Broadway Ballads for Guitar
24 arrangements, including: All I Ask Of You • Bewitched • I Dreamed A Dream • Memory • My Funny Valentine • What I Did For Love • and more.
00698984.................................$10.95

Classic Blues for Voice and Fingerstyle Guitar
20 arrangements with guitar accompaniment and solos, including: Mercury Blues • Seventh Son • Little Red Rooster • Trouble In Mind • Nobody Knows You When You're Down And Out • and more.
00698992.................................$12.95

Contemporary Movie Songs For Solo Guitar
24 arrangements of silver screen gems, including: Endless Love • The John Dunbar Theme ("Dances With Wolves") • Theme From "Ordinary People" • Somewhere Out There • Unchained Melody • and more. Includes notes and tab.
00698982.................................$14.95

Disney Fingerstyle Guitar
14 fun favorites, including: Under The Sea • Beauty And The Beast • A Whole New World • Can You Feel The Love Tonight • and more.
00690009.................................$12.95

Gospel Favorites For Fingerstyle Guitar
25 classics, including: Amazing Grace • Because He Lives • El Shaddai • How Great Thou Art • The Old Rugged Cross • Rock Of Ages • Will The Cradle Be Unbroken • Wings Of A Dove • and more. Includes notes and tab.
00698991.................................$12.95

International Favorites
25 songs that span the globe, including: Au Clair de la Lune • The Blue Bells Of Scotland • La Cucaracha • Londonderry Air • Santa Lucia • and more.
00698996.................................$12.95

Mannheim Steamroller - Christmas For Fingerstyle Guitar
Enjoy these world-famous Christmas arrangements from the best-selling Mannheim Steamroller albums. 10 pieces, including: Carol Of The Birds • The Holly And The Ivy • I Saw Three Ships • Wassail, Wassail • and more. Includes notes and tab.
00650042.................................$12.95

Fingerpicking Beatles
20 favorites, including: And I Love Her • Eleanor Rigby • Here Comes The Sun • Here, There And Everywhere • Hey Jude • Michelle • Norwegian Wood • While My Guitar Gently Weeps • Yesterday • and more.
00699404.................................$14.95

Eric Clapton Fingerstyle Guitar Collection
12 Clapton classics for fingerstyle guitar. Includes: Bell Bottom Blues • Cocaine • Layla • Nobody Knows You When You're Down And Out • Strange Brew • Tears In Heaven • Wonderful Tonight • and 5 more favorites.
00699411.................................$10.95

A Fingerstyle Guitar Christmas
29 great fingerstyle arrangements, including: Angels We Have Heard On High • Auld Lang Syne • The First Noel • Good King Wenceslas • The Holly And The Ivy • Jingle Bells • O Little Town Of Bethlehem • Up On The Housetop • What Child Is This? • and more.
00699038.................................$12.95

Billy Joel - The Fingerstyle Collection
15 of his most popular hits arranged for fingerstyle guitar, including: Honesty • Just The Way You Are • My Life • Piano Man • Uptown Girl • and more.
00699410.................................$12.95

Elton John - The Fingerstyle Collection
15 fingerstyle arrangements, including: Your Song • Daniel • Bennie And The Jets • Crocodile Rock • Don't Go Breaking My Heart • Candle In The Wind • and more. Includes notes and tab.
00699414.................................$14.95

TV Tunes For Guitar
23 fingerstyle arrangements of America's most memorable TV themes, including: The Addams Family • The Brady Bunch • Coach • Frasier • Happy Days • Hill Street Blues • I Love Lucy • Mister Ed • Northern Exposure • The Odd Couple • St. Elsewhere • and more.
00698985.................................$12.95

For More Information, See Your Local Music Dealer, Or Write To:

Hal•Leonard Corporation
7777 W. Bluemound Rd. P.O. Box 13819 Milwaukee, WI 53213
http://www.halleonard.com

Prices, contents, and availability subject to change without notice. Some products may not be available outside the U.S.A.

Classical Guitar Publications

FROM

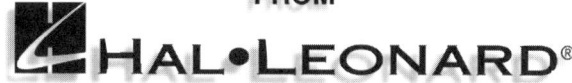

A Modern Approach to Classical Guitar
by Charles Duncan
This multi-volume method was developed to allow students to study the art of classical guitar within a new, more contemporary framework. For private, class or self-instruction. Book One features an all-new format that incorporates chord frames and symbols, as well as a record to assist in tuning and to provide accompaniments for at-home practice. Book One also introduces beginning fingerboard technique and music theory. Book Two and Three build upon the techniques learned in Book One.
00695119 Composite (Contains Books One, Two and Three) Book/CD Pack $24.95

A Modern Approach to Classical Repertoire
by Charles Duncan
A graded anthology of solo pieces (easy to intermediate) that serves as a supplement to Books Two and Three of *A Modern Approach to Classical Guitar*.
00699204 Part One Book Only......................$7.95
00699208 Part Two Book Only $7.95

Twenty Studies For Guitar
Sor/Segovia
We've added a demonstration recording to this traditional, standard guitar book. The recordings done by Paul Henry are extremely helpful to teachers and students. Each study is completely recorded.
00006362 Book/Cassette Pack $14.95
00006363 Book Only................................$6.95
00695012 Book/CD Pack..........................$17.95

Matteo Carcassi – 25 Melodic and Progressive Studies, Op. 60
One of Carcassi's (1792-1853) most famous collections of classical guitar music – indispensable for the modern guitarist's musical and technical development. Available with CD or cassette, performed by Paul Henry. 49-minute audio accompaniment.
00696505 Book/Cassette Pack $14.95
00696506 Book/CD Pack..........................$17.95

Julio S. Sagreras – First Lessons for Guitar
One of the world's most popular beginning classical guitar methods by South American guitar virtuoso Julio Sagreras and translated by Bernard Moore. Features carefully sequenced studies covering technique and theory through music etudes and pieces.
50010310 Volume 1......................$6.95
50010320 Volume 2......................$6.95

Beatles for Classical Guitar
More than 25 of the Beatles greatest hits arranged for classical guitar, including: Here Comes the Sun • In My Life • The Long and Winding Road • Things We Said Today • Yesterday • more.
00699073......................................$12.95

Liona Boyd – A Guitar For Christmas
19 favorite Christmas songs arranged for classical guitar. Songs include: Silent Night • O Come All Ye Faithful • The First Noel • Away In A Manger.
00699070 ....$9.95

Liona Boyd – Miniatures for Guitar
A charming collection of shorter compositions for the classical guitar arranged and fingered by one of today's outstanding artists.
00699385 Book/Cassette Pack $14.95
00699386 Book/CD Pack............................$17.95

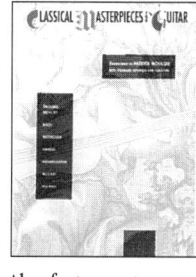

Classical Masterpieces for Guitar
27 works by Bach, Beethoven, Handel, Mendelssohn, Mozart and more transcribed with standard notation and tablature. Now anyone can enjoy classical material regardless of their guitar background. Also features stay-open binding.
00699312....................................$12.95

Great Composers for Guitar
14 pieces by the most famous composers of all time, arranged by Leon Block for solo guitar. These arrangements are intended for the intermediate fingerstyle or flat-picking guitarist. Includes: Clair de lune (Debussy) • Cordoba (Lecuona) • The Harmonious Blacksmith (Handel) • Sonata L. 423 (Scarlatti) • and more.
00699048..................................$5.95

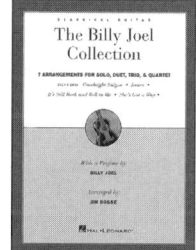

The Billy Joel Collection
arranged by Jim Bosse preface by Billy Joel
7 arrangements for solo, duet, trio and quartet. Includes: The Downeaster "Alexa" (solo) • Goodnight Saigon (duet) • It's Still Rock and Roll to Me (trio) • Lullabye (solo) • She's Got a Way (solo) • and more.
00699114..................................$12.95

Andrew Lloyd Webber – The Classical Guitar Collection
22 Lloyd Webber classics from his very best shows, including: Close Every Door • I Don't Know How to Love Him • Don't Cry for Me Argentina • Memory • Unexpected Song • Pie Jesu • All I Ask of You • Love Changes Everything • and more.
00699346................................$9.95

The Genius of Django Reinhardt
This classic collection of Django tunes is an intimate look at his style. Included are transcriptions of many Django tunes complete with all rhythm guitar changes. Included are: Crepuscule • Belleville • Are You in the Mood • Ultra Fox • and 14 others. As a bonus we've included special chorus arrangements to four tunes arranged by Ike Issacs in the style of Django. These include: My Serenade • Minor Swing • Manoir De Mes Reves • and Daphne.
00026711 ....$10.95

FOR MORE INFORMATION, SEE YOUR LOCAL MUSIC DEALER, OR WRITE TO:

7777 W. BLUEMOUND RD. P.O. BOX 13819 MILWAUKEE, WI 53213
http://www.halleonard.com

Prices, contents, and availability subject to change without notice.
Some products may not be available outside the U.S.A.

0299

THE PUBLICATIONS OF
CHRISTOPHER PARKENING

THE CHRISTOPHER PARKENING GUITAR METHOD, VOL. 1 – REVISED
in collaboration with
Jack Marshall and David Brandon
Learn the art of the classical guitar with this premier method for beginners by one of the world's preeminent virtuosos and the recognized heir to the legacy of Andrés Segovia. Learn basic classical guitar technique by playing beautiful pieces of music, including over 50 classical pieces, 26 exercises, and 14 duets. Includes notes in the first position, how to hold the guitar, tuning, right and left hand technique, arpeggios, tone production, placement of fingers and nails, flats, naturals, key signatures, the bar, and more. Also includes many helpful photos and illustrations, plus sections on the history of the classical guitar, selecting a guitar, guitar care, and more.
00695228...$12.95

THE CHRISTOPHER PARKENING GUITAR METHOD, VOL. 2
Intermediate to Upper-Intermediate Level
Continues where Vol. 1 leaves off. Teaches: all notes in the upper position; tone production; advanced techniques such as tremolo, harmonics, vibrato, pizzicato and slurs; practice tips; stylistic interpretation; and more. The first half of the book deals primarily with technique, while the second half of the book applies the technique with repertoire pieces. As a special bonus, this book includes 32 previously unpublished Parkening edition pieces by composers including Dowland, Bach, Scarlatti, Sor, Tarrega and other, plus three duets for two guitars.
00695229...$12.95

PARKENING AND THE GUITAR – VOL. 1
Music of Two Centuries:
Popular New Transcriptions for Guitar
Virtuoso Music for Guitar
Ten transcriptions for solo guitar of beautiful music from many periods and styles, edited and fingered by Christopher Parkening. All pieces are suitable for performance by the advanced guitarist. Ten selections: Afro-Cuban Lullaby • Empress of the Pagodes (Ravel) • Menuet (Ravel) • Minuet in D (Handel) • Passacaille (Weiss) • Pastourelle (Poulenc) • Pavane for a Dead Princess (Ravel) • Pavane for a Sleeping Beauty (Ravel) • Preambulo (Scarlatti-Ponce) • Sarabande (Handel).
00699105...$9.95

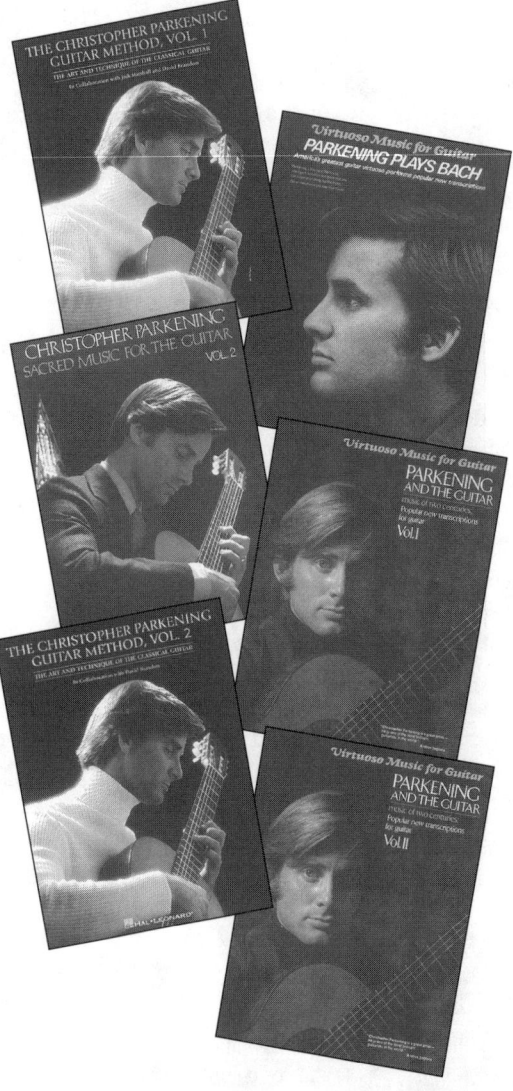

PARKENING AND THE GUITAR – VOL. 2
Music of Two Centuries: Popular New Transcriptions for Guitar
Virtuoso Music for Guitar
Nine more selections for the advanced guitarist: Clair de Lune (Debussy) • Giga (Visée) • The Girl with the Flaxen Hair (Debussy) • Gymnopedie Nos. I-III (Satie) • The Little Shepherd (Debussy) • The Mysterious Barricades (Couperin) • Sarabande (Debussy).
00699106...$9.95

CHRISTOPHER PARKENING – SACRED MUSIC FOR THE GUITAR, VOL. 1
Seven inspirational arrangements, transcriptions and compositions covering traditional Christian melodies from several centuries. These selections appear on the Parkening album Sacred Music for the Guitar. Includes: Präludium (Bach) • Our Great Savior • God of Grace and God of Glory (2 guitars) • Brethren, We Have Met to Worship • Deep River • Jesus, We Want to Meet • Evening Prayer.
00699095...$10.95

CHRISTOPHER PARKENING – SACRED MUSIC FOR THE GUITAR, VOL. 2
Seven more selections from the album Sacred Music for the Guitar: Hymn of Christian Joy (guitar and harpsichord) • Simple Gifts • Fairest Lord Jesus • Stir Thy Church, O God Our Father • All Creatures of Our God and King • Glorious Things of Thee Are Spoken • Praise Ye the Lord (2 guitars).
00699100...$10.95

PARKENING PLAYS BACH
Virtuoso Music for Guitar
Nine transcriptions edited and fingered by Parkening: Preludes I, VI & IX • Gavottes I & II • Jesu, Joy of Man's Desiring • Sheep May Safely Graze • Wachet Auf, Ruft Uns Die Stemme • Be Thou with Me • Sleepers Awake (2 guitars).
00699104...$9.95

"Parkening's playing of Bach is so intelligent, sensitive and adept that one can forget everything but the music."
– The New York Times

CHRISTOPHER PARKENING – ROMANZA
Virtuoso Music for Guitar
Three wonderful transcriptions edited and fingered by Parkening: Catalonian Song • Rumores de la Caleta • Romance.
00699103...$7.95

For More Information, See Your Local Music Dealer,
Or Write To:

7777 W. Bluemound Rd. P.O. Box 13819 Milwaukee, WI 53213

Prices, contents and availability subject to change without notice.